Hairpreneur Hair Guide:
How To Start A Hair Business

ARTISHA L. MOORE

ii

DEDICATION

I would like to dedicate this book to my husband and children. Without them, I would have not taken the struggles and obstacles that I have taken to get this far. To my support team and clients, without you all, I wouldn't have anything to write about. Also to my mentor Tamara Garrison, I cannot thank you enough. You all have made this journey something that I will never forget.

CONTENTS

ACKNOWLEDGMENTS

I want to start by thanking my wonderful husband Demetrius for believing in my multiple visions of starting my hair business. I also want to give a huge thank you to my children, Zariah and Steven. Because of them, I continue to show them that success is what you make of it. Also, a grateful and humble thank you to my supporters. Without you all, I wouldn't have made it this far. You all are wonderful.

1 THE BEGINNING

Her name is Artisha Moore and she is the owner and founder of Artisha's Hair and Beauty Bar. She started her hair business in June of 2017, with the vision and a dream. Let's start at the beginning. She was raised around cosmetologist all of her life. As a kid growing up in Detroit, Michigan; she use to sit and watch her grandmother do her client's hair. She would mimic her by using dolls to try to create the same look as her grandmother was doing. In her teens, her aunt would have her help around in the salon (especially when Artisha wanted a new hairstyle); by prepping her clients so she can do their hair. Her aunt taught her a lot when it came to different hair textures, hairstyles, what products to use, what products are good or bad for the hair, and what could damage the hair follicles.

Since then, she has always loved the beauty of hair. How it flows, how it can mold into whatever hairstyle want it to do. In middle school, Artisha would always have a different hairstyle. Every week, her aunt would do something different to her hair. Artisha loved to be different. She expressed this through her hair. With her aunt teaching her how to braid and to do sew-ins with extensions she grew to love hair. The expression of how a new hairstyle could transform a person inside and out to make them feel good about themselves, helped Artisha to realize that; " hair is the crown that you wear, so you better wear it well." Hair can make a person feel beautiful. With that, her passion for hair grew. The love for hair and doing hair grew inside of her.

The reason why she started her hair business at, Artisha's Hair and Beauty Bar was because she loves the technique of making hair extension looks natural. She started watching, "Mad about Meechie" on YouTube. Who is a beautiful, successful black woman who owns a hair salon and barbershop, which also has her own hair products, and hair extensions called Posh Hair. Artisha watched every one of her videos. She fell in love with her technique of doing hair and saw how successful and professional Meechie was. She gave Artisha the confidence that she can do this too and she did just that. Knowing that she had a vision similar to hers, but wasn't sure if she would get the success that she had adventured. Artisha changed her mindset and got to work and that's when she created Artisha's Hair and Beauty Bar.

One day she was scrolling through Instagram, and she came across this company (whom I will not name) they were looking for people that wanted to sell hair and make some money. Like everyone does, she googled them to read some reviews. Then she thought to herself, and said, "Ok let me sign up." So she signed up. She started selling their hair extensions. Then she noticed, "like wait a min", people are purchasing all of this hair, spending all of this money and all I get is $24 in return, but if I sell so much and hit a certain mark then I will receive a $100 bonus to use in the store. So she started thinking to herself like "Nah" She was still focusing on how much money people were spending and how much she was receiving. So one day she was on Instagram again, and she came across a shared post that belonged to Mane Elementz. She started following her. She saw that she had a membership special going on and she remembers telling her husband, and he was like, "here is my card now go sign up." So she did! She followed everything that Mane Elementz had posted. Artisha went to every training, she followed every rule, wrote down everything that Mane Elementz was teaching. Artisha started to follow her Facebook page because Mane Elementz gave so much education and knowledge that Artisha began her journey on becoming a Hairpreneur.

Later on, in that same year of 2017, not even six months into her new journey, Artisha's Hair Bar got voted for the number one Hair

Extension Company in Texas. By paying attention to her customer needs and by providing exceptional and honest customer service, Artisha's Hair Bar has grown fast in this online industry.

Now a year later, after paying attention to everything that she has learned, she has now become affiliated with some great entrepreneur women from all over the world. She has started networking with some people out in LA, collaborating with some Youtubers, she is launching her YouTube channel, and in 2019 she will be opening up her store, as well as becoming a wholesaler. The first year of opening up any business will be a migraine because of the concept of learning how to become a BOSS. It is like learning how to tie a shoe. Just keep trying even when that knot falls, you may pout, or cry, but keep trying until that knot stay! That is what Artisha did. She wanted to give up so many times, but she kept tying that shoe until it stayed. So don't give up. Keep trying. People are always watching. That person may be the one who will become the mentor that will guide and give you the strength that is needed and that will give you all of the steps that are needed to be successful in your new journey. CHANG YOUR MINDSET.

2 GETTING STARTED

Getting started as a Hairpreneur or in any entrepreneur business, change your mindset of thinking. Think about your vision and your goals. Write them down so you can begin your journey. Once you have changed your mindset and you have set your vision and goals. Next, think of a name for your business; make sure your name is usable by running it through the USPTO database. Once your name has cleared, GET LEGAL! Get your name trademarked. Learn the difference between a trademark and patent. Figure out if you will have an LLC, Corp, or a DBA for your business. These are all important to know when going into business for yourself. Figure out if you will have employees or not. Get your EIN with the IRS.

Create your business plan. In that business plan, you need to know who your target audience will be. Will it be women, men or both? What age groups are you targeting? Who is your competition?

Don't look at the word competition as one, but look at the phrase competition as to how your product will be different from that company. What are you going to bring to the company that is going to make you stand out? What are your target sales? How much are you trying to make in a day, week, month, and year? You have to set these goals so you can be successful. Learning time management, get you a log book so you can stay organized. These are some glimpse of what I did to get started in my business.

When she started Artisha's Hair and Beauty Bar, she did not have the inventory on hand at that time. She shopped around for vendors to receive samples of products that I wanted and chose the company that I felt had the best for my buck. All I had were samples of my products for people to see, touch, and feel. Eventually, my vendor provided a drop shipping company that held my entire inventory. So depending on what you want for your hair business needs, think about the stock. Are you going to have inventory on hand or will you have it, someone, to drop ship your products for you? There are a lot of things to think about when starting a business.

Before she started Artisha's Hair & Beauty Bar, she worked for another company selling hair for them. Seeing that she was making pennies on a dollar, while they were making the big bank off of her selling their product she said, "No." It was time for her to start her hair business. So she connected with Mane Elementz, followed her plan, and started her hair business. Mane Elementz made it so easy to understand, but she also made it known that your first year will not be easy, you will not become rich overnight, and if you are looking for a get rich scheme, then this is not for you. Starting a hair business is much work. People think that having an online store is easy. It looks easy, but the task of everyday processes is very challenging.

There are many obstacles that you will encounter. Sometimes you will feel like the support is not there, but it is. It's just not from the people you wish it were from. You will learn that the people whom you may love or even the people you have known for over twenty years will not be your first supporters, they may never support you, but that is ok. You would rather be around people who genuinely love you or love what you are doing. Artisha came in contact with people that do not know her personally but supports her like they have known her all of her life.

Mane Elementz made sure that everyone knew and understood the hair business. She did not sugarcoat anything, but the main thing that she made sure of was how the hair business worked. This made it easy for me to understand and made it easy for me to identify that there will be some mistakes, misleading people, losing friends, and a lot more obstacles along the way. You will also meet some great people to network with as well.

3 PROS AND CONS

There are pros and cons in the hair business, but what company doesn't have those issues? The advantages and disadvantages of being a Hairpreneur break even. The whole propose of coming into a market of your own is that you want to be your boss. Not knowing all of the issues about customers service that comes along with this, but you have to be able to identify and understand these issues; know how to address these issues, and how to fix them. Yes, you will have your good and bad days; you will struggle with trying to figure out why this customer wants a refund or how to complete a chargeback. You will have to set goals and learn from these mistakes so your business can grow so you can be successful. If a business did not experience the "cons," then every company would be perfect.

The best thing about having your own business is that you are your boss. You do not have to worry about calling in if you're sick, if you want to take some time off for a vacation don't have to worry about waking up on time so you won't be late to someone else job. You are your boss, you wake up when you want to, go to bed when you feel like it, go on vacation on your time and most of all you do not have to take orders from someone else that is going to make their company rich while you are sitting making pennies on the dollars. I am not downing an everyday 9-5 job, but people complain every day about how they do not like their job, they hate their job, or they are just tired of working for someone else. Well, you are the only one who can change that, by changing your mindset. Become your boss. Stop depending on someone else to write your paycheck. Stop being the employee and become the employer. Become that entrepreneur and start your trend.

Now there are a lot of cons of in the hair business, but don't let that stop you from progressing to become your boss. There will be late nights, you will feel like giving up, there will be a lot of competition, and you will even feel like you're not going to make it. You will lose a lot of friends in this process, but don't worry about them. They were taken out for a reason. There will be people trying to tell you that you don't know what you are doing, even asking why are you doing this. There will be a lot of obstacles that will enter in your way. You will have a lot of nights when you cry because you are trying to figure out why are these people who you thought that loved you are treating you this way. There will be a lot of why's and how's. But I promise you will get over a lot them. Trust me; it comes with the territory of being a business owner.

When people start to see or think that you are doing well, they will begin to ask for money even free products. You will hear all of the stories in the world so that you can feel sorry for their situation. You will have some jealous people asking why you haven't put them on and why aren't you looking out for your people. You can't look out for everyone; everyone is not meant to be put on. You will people support you behind the scenes because they don't want "their circle" to see that they are purchasing from you. All of this is ok; take it as a thank you and investment into your company.

There will be so much that will have you drained, but you will have to learn how to block those people out. They are not worth your happiness because they are bitter about your success and where you are going in your life. You will also get a lot of "no's" before you get that one, yes, but that is ok, because that one yes may be your deal breaker. That one yes may be the golden ticket for your company. That yes maybe your 6 or 7 figure income that may just set you for life. So it is ok to get that no. Just DON'T GIVE UP, you got this.

4 DON'T GIVE UP

Giving up is so easy for us to do. When things do not feel right, we give up. When things do not go our way, we give up. Giving up should never be on our priority list, but somehow it always show. There were times when I felt like giving up and throwing in the towel. There were times when I said, "I don't care, I quit," but I didn't because in my heart I knew this is what I wanted. Giving up is easier to do then to try. When we try, it feels like a lot of work. We all know, to get what we really want, we have to put in the work, but yet we are so fast on "giving up." You defiantly have to change your mindset of thinking to get what you want. Nothing will ever be handed or given to us. Although we all would love for someone to inherit their financials to us, but we know life doesn't work like that.

So what do you do so you don't give up? You change your mindset. This is a must do process. If having your own business, not having to wake up and having to rush to someone else's employment to make them rich while you are still trying to make ends meet, you have to change your mindset of thinking. Taking some "me time" to meditate and pray every morning and in the evening will give you the strength that you need to sew into your new beginnings. The only thing you should be giving up on is making others rich. I don't know how many people love to get up every morning, to make other people rich. I know I am not one of them. Start manifesting into yourself, set aside some time to start your business plan.

Try being open to new things, find out what works for you. There is this quote that I love by Phillip Sweet that say, "***Stay true to yourself, yet always be open to learn. Work hard, and never*** *give up on your dreams, even when nobody else believes they can come true but you. These are not clichés but real tools you need no matter what you do in life to stay focused on your path."* Never give up on your dreams to satisfy someone else's life or their dreams. Sometimes it may feel like no one believes in you, but that is ok. Your dreams and your future are not for everyone to like or love. It is up to you to like and love what you are trying to accomplish. I had to learn that the hard way. Everyone is not going to be accepting your new life that you are creating.

It is time for you to take a step back and think to yourself, "what am I doing?" I remember when I was in the "thoughts" of giving up on my new adventure of becoming a Hairpreneur. I was so upset because I felt like all of my "friends" should be supporting my new adventure. When I saw that they were not supporting me that hurt me the most. I was in a state of wow!!! I saw that they were supporting and sharing other people's post or their new beginnings but not once did they do the same for me. You will come across a lot of things that will put you in the state of 'wow," but its ok, I promise. This will make you stronger. This will build you up in ways that you did not know that you had the tools to even create. I learned that everyone will not support you, and the people that you thought no matter what had your back. Just don't let them be the ones you validate the reason you gave up, but let them be the validation on why you went even harder.

The reasons why people give up. Let me tell you a few reasons why. One of the number one reasons is that, they thought this was going to be an easy journey. Let me tell you, there are bumps all through this entrepreneur life. This is one of the hardest jobs you will ever do in your lifetime. Nothing can compare to becoming an entrepreneur. I don't care how many degrees you have, the training you may have, and entrepreneurship is one of the hardest jobs ever. Another reason why people give up so easy is because; they may not have a good support system. This is where a lot of people go wrong within themselves. We look for validation from everywhere but ourselves. This is something that has to change. You have to change your mindset of thinking. The only support or validation that you need is YOU! You are the only one that matters. This new life is for you, not for everyone else. The last reason why people give up so easy is because of money. They say money rules the world, but it doesn't. What a lot of people don't know is that, you do not need a lot of money to start a business. Yes it would be great to have thousands of dollars to start off with to make sure you have everything that you need, but the people who really want it, will take money from each paycheck to create their empire. Don't let money be the reason why you haven't started your new life as an entrepreneur.

Don't block your blessings on becoming something great. Find ways to build your foundation. I mention before, I did not have a lot of money when I started my hair business. I started my business with a two dollar membership and a five dollar website. As I continued to grow in my business, then I started buying more into it. I upgraded my website started investing more into my inventory. Now like everybody else, yes I wanted to start off big, but I'm glad I didn't. I wanted to make sure that I wasn't going to lose money. I didn't want to invest in a lot of inventory and then lose a huge profit because I couldn't sell my items. So I started out small. In the beginning it wasn't going as good as I wanted it to. I wanted to sell every day, I wanted to make a profit every day, but it didn't work like that. I was new to the business, I was new to the scene, and I had to build trust within my company so people could buy and support my business. My mentor told me from the very beginning that this will not be easy. You have to build customer's trust. I still felt like the people that were supposed to be my friends, I just knew they were going to be my support to help me build my customers trust. Again, I wanted to just give up. I wanted my business to jump off in the beginning. I wanted my business to be well known because my name was attached to it. But, I never gave up. I kept going and I kept finding ways to improve my business. You cannot let friends or family be the reasons why you give up. The only person that is standing in your way is yourself. You are your only failure on why you did not complete your new journey. Stop blaming others for your "why nots".

5 FINDING A VENDOR

The tricky part about being in business for yourself is finding a vendor that you can trust. There are a lot of vendors out there that is trying to get your business. This is how they continue to get business as well. It's a cycle of repeated customers, because no matter what, you the buyer and supplier is still a customer.

I can't express enough, DO YOUR RESEARCH!! You cannot just jump on the first vendor you see and start purchasing from them. Shop around; buy some samples before you just go with that one vendor. Just because the product looks good in a picture doesn't mean their quality is good. Trust me; you will go through a lot of vendors before you find that one you can trust. Also, do you know what type of hair that you want to sell? Are you selling virgin hair, processed hair, unprocessed hair? Do you know the difference between the hairs that you want to sell? What origin? What grade of hair do you want to sell? Do you know the difference between the hairs grades that you want to sell? There are so many things that you need to know before finding the best vendor that will supply you with everything that you needing for your business. I will supply you with the steps that you need to finding a hair vendor that you can trust and that will supply your goods for a good price.

1. You want to understand your industry first. Understanding and educating yourself on your business will help lead you to the vendors that may be the best fit for you. Remember you are looking for wholesale prices. If your wholesale price looks like a retail price, you may want to do more research into that company or move on to the next.

2. Try out their product. Ask the vendor to supply you with some samples. Some vendors will supply the samples, but the shipping maybe way too expensive. Depending where it is coming from. Also

ask them if the samples you are receiving are they full bundles or pieces of bundles. It is best to get a full bundle that way you can get the real feel of the hair that you may purchase with them in the future.

3. Get in contact with the wholesaler. Once you have received your goods, contact the wholesaler and start business with them. Once they see that you are serious, a lot of them will work out deals that will benefit you and your business.

4. Try researching a wholesaler on google. There are a lot of hair vendors out there, but always do your research before purchasing a full product with that company. Go to YouTube and research videos from that supplier. There are a lot of honest people you do testimonials on these companies. Just remember, you cannot take their word for it every time., But you do want to take into consideration if this was their first purchase or did something happen between those two parties on why they gave a bad review.

5. Try subscribing to trade publications. You can find these in magazines and online newsletters. You want to stay in touch with your chosen industry. Products change every day.

6. Attend hair shows. A lot of these hair show sponsors are wholesale vendors as well.

7. Don't be scare to mess up. Your first wholesale supplier may not be your lifelong vendor. Creating your perfect supply chain is an evolution involving a lot of trial and error. Remember, all you need from your first supplier is a product that you can ship at a profit. It may not be the best wholesale price for you, but don't sweat that in the beginning. Your first goal is to ship product. Then you can improve your bottom line by trying other wholesale suppliers.

Now that you have a little better understanding on what to look for when finding a vendor I hope this will lead you into the right direction. I know how hard it is to find a vendor that will supply your needs for your company. The best thing that you could ever do is get you a plane ticket and travel to those suppliers to see firsthand how your future product is created. That way you can see and feel the hair for yourself.

Be careful with these hair vendors online. Social media vendors are one of the ones that will get you for your dollar. Not saying that all of them are bad or out to get your money, but you should be very careful. Research them; see if they have a website that you can review. See if they have any reviews on their site. You have to research before you just jump right in on these vendors. They are out to make money just like you. The only difference is that once you sell one bad bundle to a customer, that one bad hair sell can change your company. You have to know how to deal with issues like this because they will arise. Just like vendors, your customers will try to ruin you. All you need is one bad review that will go viral and that can tarnish your name. So make sure you are providing great quality products with great quality customer service.

6 WHAT DO YOU KNOW ABOUT HAIR

What do you know about the hair you are selling? In the beginning I had no idea about the different types of hair. I didn't know about the grades, the origin, and the difference between processed and unprocessed hair, if it was good hair or bad hair. All I knew was that I love hair and that I wanted to sell it. I just wanted to have my own business and selling hair online was booming and I wanted a part of that pie.

After learning that there are so many types of hair out there, I knew I had to sit down and educate myself on this business or I was going to fail at this new journey. My mentor would always keep me up to date on what's good and what's not. I purchased a few of her books to educate myself on what I knew was going to be my new life. People think selling hair is easy. Well I'm here to tell you it's not. Especially if you do not know what you are selling. Any business that you go into you need to know where it came from. How was it created? Did the hair come from a donor, there are so many things that you need to know, because there is a hair guru out there that is ready to test you about your business to see what you really know. If someone comes up to you and ask you what type of hair is this and all you can say is that its Brazilian body wave, you better be ready to break that down. They may ask what grade of hair it is, they may ask if it's processed or not. Is it virgin hair, is it raw hair. You need to be ready because this is your business and you need to know what you are selling.

This is why it is good to start out small when it comes to selling hair. It is good to specialize in a certain area until you get the roll down of being a Hairpreneur. Think of what type of hair you want to specialize in. Meaning, are you going to specialize in just raw hair extensions, processed hair extensions, Indian hair extensions, are you going to specialize in just wigs, if so what type: human hair or synthetic. There are so many types of hair out there; you have to research your business before just jumping into everything right away.

If a customer comes up to you ask you what type of hair would be best to blend in with my hair, will you be able to tell them and show them the correct hair? If someone ask you what type of extensions do you carry? Will you be able to tell them that your hair is 100% human hair if so what type? Is your hair Remy Hair? If so what type? There are a lot of things to take into consideration when selling hair. If someone were to ask you where do you get your hair from? Will you be able to tell them? The most common places are India and Europe. If you're a brunette or want to add volume, Indian hair is your best bet. If you're blonde or have finer hair, European is a better fit (though a bit pricier). You have to know your product before you just jump out there and say that you are a Hairpreneur.

Know what products works best for your hair is also a good know service. How will you tell your customers to care for their hair? I provide hair care instructions for my hair, so my customers will know exactly what to use on their bundles. The goal is for your bundles to last for a long a time. So know what products best fits your business needs is very important.

(Hair care tip: Using products that are free from harsh chemicals is a good source. If you won't put it on your natural hair, don't use it on your bundles.)

You want to prolong the life of your extensions, so keeping them free from tangling is the number one source. When you sleep, wrap your hair into a loose braid or ballerina bun, which will prevent hair from rubbing against your pillow and knotting. Also wrapping your hair in a silk or satin scarf will keep it in good condition. Use a leave-in conditioner spray; this will keep your bundles from knots. To combat the inevitable tangles, use a paddle brush to brush your bundles. This will help detangle the hair safely. And, lastly, hair extensions take longer to dry than regular hair because they've been processed and hold onto moisture, so a good blow dryer will help you save time all of this information is great to know so you can tell your customers on how to care for their hair. You want your customers to continue to come to you for their haircare needs and wants. If you don't provide this information to your customers and they start to use or just anything to their hair, their outcome is going to turn into your income, meaning when their hair starts to tangle and get matted, they are going to blame you for not giving the hair care instructions that they needed to take care of their bundles. So if you want their outcome to increase your income, know your hair so you can provide great customer care to every customer so they can continue to come back and bring more customers to you.

7 SOCIAL MEDIA

Social Media is one of the leading platforms for business and marketing. There are good and bad things about doing business on social media.

Doing business on social media has taken over the world. Your store front is at everyone's fingertips once they log in. Everyone can see what you are doing when it comes to social media. So if you are doing business on the internet, make sure you provide content that is going to continue to catch the eyes of your potential customers. Learn how to use this platform as an advantage to you and your company. Pay attention to other companies that are using social media to market their products. What do they have that you don't is the question to ask yourself. How can you mimic that marketing but make it your own. You don't want to display the same content as the next so discover a way to make your marketing different than the others. Here are some examples to give you an idea on how to market your products.

1. **Do some behind the scenes**. People love to see what you are doing. Show them how you are creating content without giving them all of the details. Do some live footage of your photoshoot with your products? Maybe provide some video snippets of what is going on with your business. Provide some really great pictures for your website and social media page. Make your photos bright and clear so people can what is happening.

2. **Have a consistent line up**. Posting everyday will keep your followers looking and waiting to see what you are doing in your business. People are going to want to follow you more based on what you post and share with the world, so make sure that you are consistent. You don't want to post too much in one day. One or two post a day will be fine.

3. **Hashtags.** Hashtags is a way of getting everyone's attention. On

Instagram, you are allowed 30 hashtags, so make those hashtags worth it. But don't overdue your hashtags, switch them. If you use the same hashtags a lot they become blacklisted and no one will see that post. So switch up your hashtags or spread them out.

Don't let social media take over your business or your thoughts on your business. We are so stuck on how many followers we have, how many likes we have that we forget that all of your sales will not always come from social media. This is where we have to reprogram ourselves and go out to different places and establishments to market our products as well. Once you put yourself out there in the public eye and make a name out of yourself, eventually more people will start to follow you. Because they will ask, "do you have Instagram"? I rarely hear people ask about Facebook. That's because it is easier to market on Instagram, but your account must be public for people to follow your hashtags to your page.

You want to create a social media that will display your marketing goals. Know who you are marketing too. So plan how you want your social media to run. Develop you a social media strategy plan. This should layout your steps on what you are marketing and who you are marketing too. Once you have that entire laid out, figure out your goals for marketing on social media. What are you trying to accomplish on this platform. In the beginning you never want to take on so many social Medias all at once. This can be very stressful if you don't have someone that can help you monitor those sites.

Writing out your social media goals will give you an idea on where you started out today and where you are now. So if your goal is to reach 500 people in the next two months, write that down and configure how you are going to do so. What are you going to do to get those 500 people? Are you going to do more live videos since that has become really popular? Figure out what you are going to do. Remember this is your business; you have to provide material that is going to catch the eyes of your potential new customers. Here are some tips that can help you achieve your social media goals from now and into the future.

1. **You want to increase your brand**. You want people to know who you are and know your brand. You want your brand to be long lasting. Don't drown your social media with unnecessary content and promotional messages; instead provide meaningful content that focuses on your brand.

2. **You want higher quality of sales.** This means, monitor and see what hashtags have been getting everyone's attention. This may be hard to do or keep up with. But visiting the explore pages on Instagram is a way to see whose on top.

3. **Research your social media audience.** See what everyone is into; see what other influencers are doing to increase their audience and

to get more followers.

4. **Know where your audience is located.** Know the demographics of your followers are always good. There are so many people overseas who do not have some of the products that we have here in the United States. Try shipping products to them; let them know that you ship any and everywhere.

There are so many things that you can do on social media to help build your business. You just have to put the work in to find out what is best for your business. In this business, you will research every day on how to improve your brand. This is something you should do every day. You want to set yourself different from everybody. You have to stick out like a sore thumb. If this is something that you really want for your future, you will do everything possible to build your brand and make it your own so people can see who you are

8 BUIILDING YOUR WEBSITE

There are a lot of programs out there that can help you build your website. That's if you're a computer savvy, if not hire someone to do it for you.

When building a website for your business, you want it to be professional; you want your website to be something to look at. You don't want your website to be too busy or cluttered with content to where people get lost and don't know what they are looking for.

Having the right amount of content on your website that will draw your customer's attention for years to come is what you want. I know us women love us some pink and glitter. It's ok to market that look on social media, but not for your website. You want your website to be clean, clear, and straight to the point.

Before building your website, you must register your domain name so you are able to create and attach it to your website. When registering your domain name, make sure it is unique. The domain generator will tell you if this domain name is available or not, so make sure you have plenty of names to choose from or different types of spellings when choosing a name for your website. Once you find a name you will be able to attach that name to your website. This name will direct people to your site to purchase items (www.artishashairbars.com). These domain names are not free; you do have to pay a small fee to purchase one.

Whoever is creating your website, you want to make sure that you have an SEO embedded into your site. That way if someone was looking for *Raw*

Indian Hair, anyone that is selling that type of hair will come up in the search engine. Building a website is not cheap. It can range from $300 to thousands of dollars, depending on what you need for your website. Unless you know how to build one on your own, or have a really close friend that wouldn't charge, I would go that route. Just make sure that you have everything you need so people can find you if they were to google a product. There are programs out there that will show you step by step on building your website. Just make sure that it is the right program for you to create the best content for your business.

9 WHAT IS YOUR AFFIRMATION

What is your AFFIRMATION? What keeps you going on a daily bases? It is good to write these down, that way you will have something to remind you of your purpose on why you do what you are doing. Sometimes we need our own personal things that we say to ourselves to keep us motivated. I know sometimes we look to others to give us that motivation. But the question is what your purpose is? I have built my affirmations on my needs. The things that I need to do to help me stay focus on the steps that I need to continue to take on a daily bases to meet my goals.

You set your affirmation to your standards. Build you a list. It's ok to add to that list every day. Let that be a part of your "me time." I set a new goal for me every day. I try my best to complete that goal to the best of my ability. You have to prepare yourself and build yourself up, because this is part of changing your mindset. Develop you a five year plan. Make it realistic. Start marking off those goals as you complete them. If you really want a change in your life, you will start to develop those goals and executing them.

With your affirmation, create your overall goal for that year. If you have a business, think about how much money you want to make that year. That way you can break down on how much money you want to make in a day, a week, a month, and when that year ends see if you made your goal. If you didn't, figure out what you did wrong. You will have to learn how to face your challenges on a daily. In this business, you will face challenges that you didn't even know existed. But you have to be ready, because this will make you readjust your mindset again.

In your affirmation, know your integrity. What does your business stand for? Make sure your business stands for something, not just that you sell hair. What does selling hair mean to you? Then you put that energy into your business and reap the benefits off of that. Once you do, create a new goal off of that. Any challenge that you face in this business, make it into a positive. Never let a challenge knock you down to where you can't redeem your success. You flip that negative into a positive and march with it heads on. You never want your customers see you breakdown. This is your business and it means something to you, so you will stand for it and with it and show people that this is not a game. This business is my affirmation. Sometimes I have to tell myself that all money isn't good money. I have returned money to people multiple of times, because you know who is really there to support you and you know those that are there to make a bad mock of what you stand for.

Always find a solution to your problem. If you have a customer that is just irate. Find a solution; maybe give them a discount off their next purchase. Find a way to satisfy that customer. Remember your business is a part of your affirmation. Your goals for your future is your gateway to success. Never let anyone stand in your way of being successful.

10 HOW TO BE SUCCESSFUL

Being successful in this business is up to you. You control your business. You control how it is going to run. This is your success.

You have to find your niche. Once you find what you are good at, turn that into your income. Never stop learning about your business. Things changes on a daily. Make sure you stay up on all of the new products that are coming out. Work on your customer service skills. How can you provide great customer service so your customers will come back and so they can tell their friends? Word of mouth is the best advertisement. So providing great customer service is the key to being successful. Learn how to market yourself. Figure out how you will get yourself known in your industry. There are thousands of online hair companies, but how are you going to stand out? Learn how to sell your products. Know who you are marketing too. Know what you are marketing. And if you are in the hair business, become a hairstylist. This will give you a lot of connections to other hairstylist that may need your services. Also, if you are a hairstylist, some people may take you more serious as well as your business.

You have to think SUCCESS. Success does not come overnight. Although we all wish it did. To be successful, you have to act, think, dress, and speak success. You can't just start a business thinking that you are going to be successful just because that industry is booming. No, you have to think about how these people got to their success. What are they doing that you haven't tried doing yet. One thing that I do know is if you don't put yourself out there so the world can see you, your brand will never be known of. This means, taking steps that you didn't know was possible. Now, if you are shy, this business is not for you. I hear all the time that, "I don't know if I can sell anything," "I'm too shy." I hear some crazy things that follow behind the words, wanting to be your own boss. But they are not trying to remove themselves from that box even try to reach out to their success. You will not find success by being trapped in that box of "I don't know." .

Another way in being successful is who you surround yourself with. You may have to leave some people behind that are not on the same page you are. That circle you so call have that's still not doing nothing but punching uncle Sam's clock but complaining about how tired they are of working for other people, may not be the person you need to hang around. Surround yourself around people who want something, who is doing things to change their mindset, and not people who always complaining.

Research and read upon entrepreneurs who started from nothing and now how they have become billionaires. You literally have to remove yourself from all of the negativity in order to be successful. Start following entrepreneurs on social media that is in the same industry as you are or that you are trying to be a part of. Start dressing like success. When you start dressing like success, people will start looking at you different, they will want to sit down do and lunch and speak business with you. Once you start feeling like success, a lot of successful things start to follow up.

How bad do you want it? I know when I started my hair business I just wanted to be successful in what I was doing, but as I really got into it and learning my business, I changed my whole success lineup. I started partnering up with other successful people. I started following their success stories. Following their dos and don'ts. Then I entered a platform, where hundreds of people were able to hear me speak about how I got started. Once I did that, I knew I was headed out for success. You never know who is listening and watching you. I have people reaching out to me to become their mentor in this business. Once that started to happen, I knew I was going on the right path to being successful.

Success is something that you earn; it is not giving to you. You have to work hard day in and day out to get where you need to be. I don't care how hard you work on your 9-5; you will never be as successful as you should be. You are limited on what you can do with that company. You cap out after so long. So that means your success is limited with that company, which means you are limiting yourself. Now think about the CEO of that company that you work for. Their success is nonstop because, now they are creating something new within their company for them to profit from. They are increasing their success by opening up a new business and you are still in the same spot. Now think of your business. You are the CEO of your business, now you are creating jobs, you are successful, and you are building an empire that is YOURS. Never limit your success based on someone else's.

ABOUT THE AUTHOR

Artisha Moore is the Founder and CEO of Artisha's Hair and Beauty Bar. She started Artisha's Hair and Beauty Bar one year ago to create a way for women to have access to all of their beauty needs for a reasonable price. Artisha has always been into hair and makeup, which prompted her to start her hair and beauty business. Her motto is; "I Have a Cocktail Full of Beauty," and that is what she provides for all of her customers. She wants them to feel beautiful inside and out!!! She was also voted Texas #1 Hair Extension Business for 2018.